My Visit the Dentist

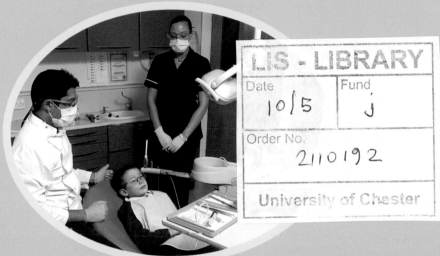

Rachel Tisdale

Photography by Chris Fairclough

W
FRANKLIN WATTS
LONDON•SYDNEY

First published in 2007 by
Franklin Watts
338 Euston Road
London NW1 3BH

Franklin Watts Australia
Level 17/207 Kent Street
Sydney NSW 2000

ISBN: 978 0 7496 7453 3 (hbk)
ISBN: 978 0 7496 7465 6 (pbk)

Dewey classification number: 617.6

A CIP catalogue record for this book is available from the British Library.

Planning and production by Discovery Books Limited
Editor: James Nixon
Designer: Ian Winton
Photography: Chris Fairclough
Series advisors: Diana Bentley MA and Dee Reid MA,
Fellows of Oxford Brookes University

The author, packager and publisher would like to thank the following
people for their participation in this book: Dr Anish K Patel and staff at the
Streatham Dental Centre, Streatham; Mrs Hunte and Jordan and Jemma Hunte.

All photographs by Chris Fairclough.

Printed in China

Franklin Watts is a division of Hachette Children's Books, an Hachette Livre UK company.

Contents

Check-up

Jordan has to visit the dentist for a check-up.

Mum phones
to make an
appointment.

At the surgery

It's time for Jordan to go to the dentist.

Jordan arrives at the dentist's surgery.

The waiting room

Jordan reads a book in the waiting room.

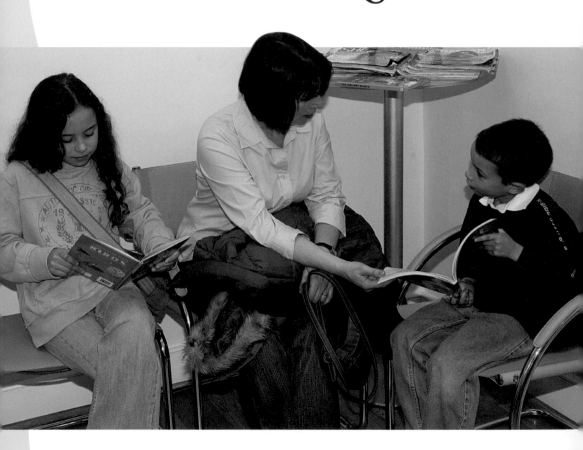

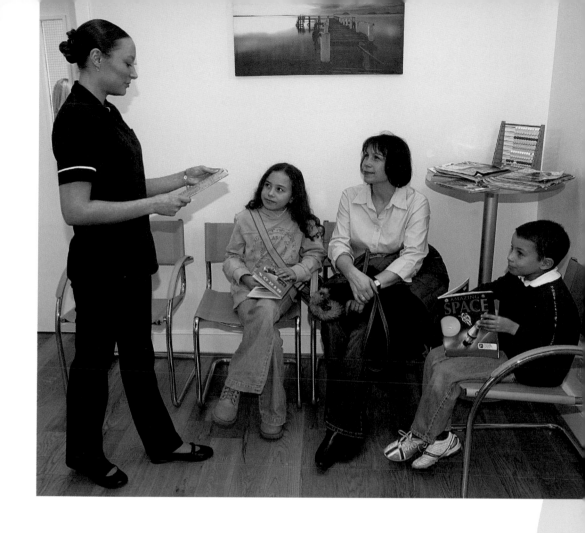

Then Jordan is called into the dentist's room.

9

The dentist's chair

Jordan sits in the chair. It moves backwards slowly.

The dentist turns on a bright light.

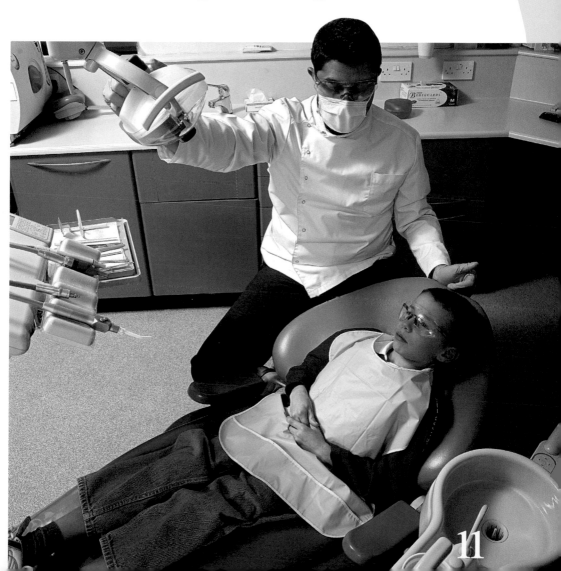

X-ray

The dentist checks
Jordan's teeth.

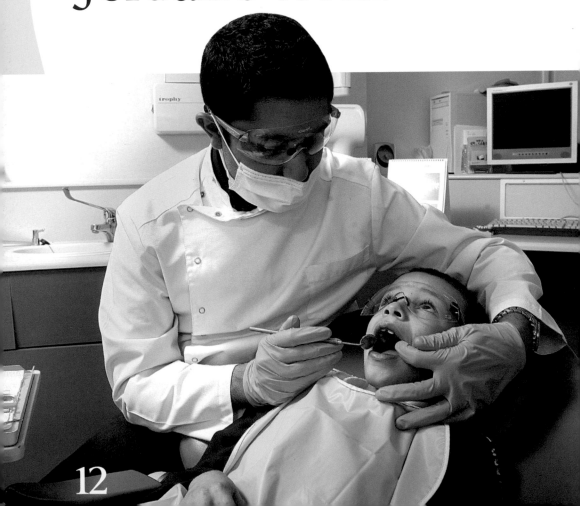

Then he takes an x-ray picture.

x-ray picture

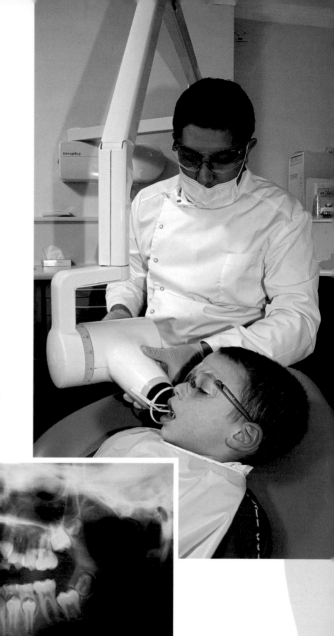

13

Dirty teeth

Jordan chews a special tablet.

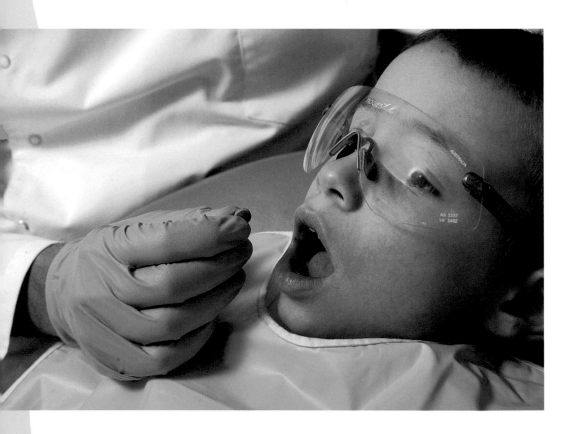

His teeth turn purple!

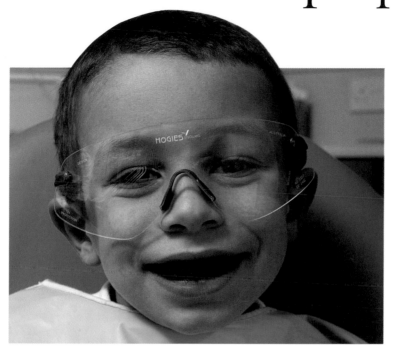

The tablet shows
where his teeth
are dirty.

Dentist's tools

The dentist uses different tools to clean Jordan's teeth.

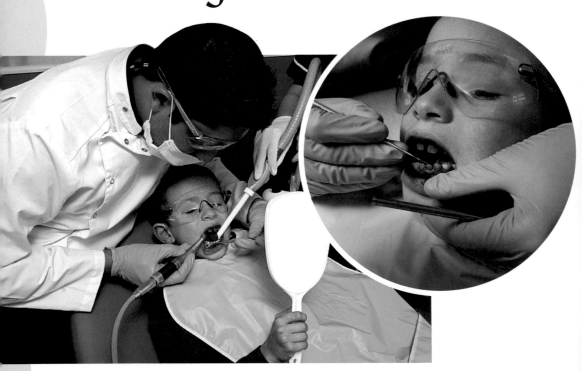

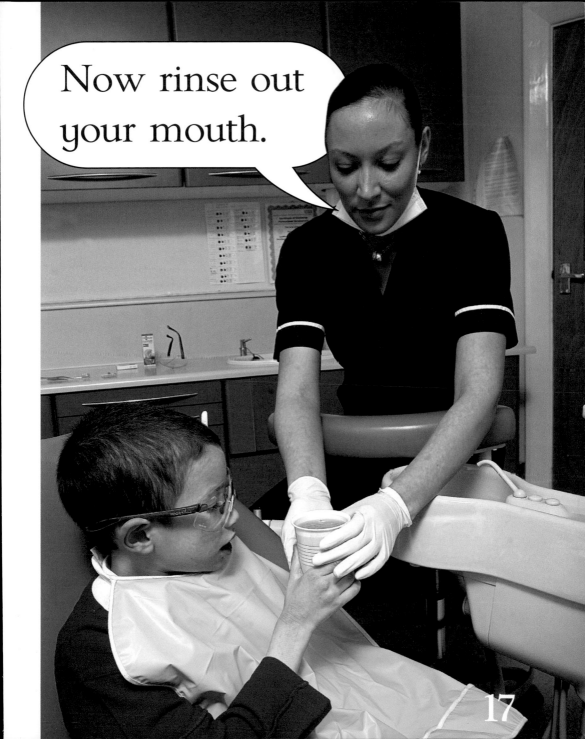

Brushing teeth

The dentist has a model of some teeth.

He shows Jordan the best way to brush.

Brush the back teeth too.

A new toothbrush

Jordan needs a new toothbrush.

He chooses an electric one.

Goodbye!

Jordan gets a sticker for being so good.

He says goodbye to the dentist.

23

Word bank

Look back for these words and pictures.

Brushing

Chair

Dentist

Light

Rinse

Tablet

Tools

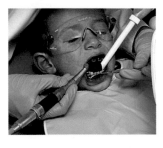

Toothbrush

X-ray

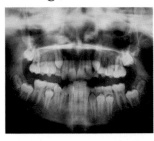